THEMATIC UNIT
Bats

Written by Jennifer Overend Prior, M. Ed.

Teacher Created Materials, Inc.
6421 Industry Way
Westminster, CA 92683
www.teachercreated.com
©1999 Teacher Created Materials, Inc.
Made in U.S.A.

ISBN-1-57690-376-1

Illustrated by
Bruce Hedges

Edited by
Janet A. Hale, M.S. Ed.

Cover Art by
Cheri Macoubrie Wilson

Table of Contents

Introduction

Bats is a captivating, language-based, thematic unit. Its 80 exciting pages are filled with a wide variety of lesson ideas designed for use with primary children. At its core are two high-quality children's literature selections, *Stellaluna* and *Zipping, Zapping, Zooming Bats*. For these books, activities are included which set the stage for reading, encourage the enjoyment of the books, and extend the concepts gained. In addition, the theme is connected to the curriculum with activities in language arts (including daily writing suggestions), math, science, social studies, art, music, and life skills. Many of these activities encourage cooperative learning. Suggestions and patterns for bulletin boards and unit-management tools are additional time savers for the busy teacher.

This thematic unit includes:

❑ **literature selections**—summaries of two children's books with related lessons (complete with reproducible pages) that cross the curriculum

❑ **poetry**—suggested selections and a poem outline enabling children to write and publish their own works

❑ **planning guides**—suggestions for sequencing lessons each day of the unit

❑ **writing ideas**—daily suggestions as well as writing activities across the curriculum, including a Big Book

❑ **bulletin board ideas**—suggestions and plans for child-created and/or interactive bulletin boards

❑ **curriculum connections**—in language arts, math, science, social studies, art, music, and life skills

❑ **group projects**—to foster cooperative learning

❑ **culminating activities**—which require children to synthesize their learning to produce a product or engage in an activity that can be shared with others

❑ **a bibliography**—suggesting additional fiction and nonfiction books on the theme, as well as educational software and educational toys

---

To keep this valuable resource intact so that it can be used year after year, you may wish to punch holes in the pages and store them in a three-ring binder.

Introduction (cont.)

Why A Balanced Approach?

The strength of a balanced language approach is that it involves children in using all modes of communication—reading, writing, listening, illustrating, and doing. Communication skills are interconnected and integrated into lessons that emphasize the whole of language. Implicit in this approach is our knowledge that every whole—including individual words—is composed of parts, and directed study of those parts can help a child to master the whole. Experience and research tell us that regular attention to phonics, other word attack skills, spelling, etc., develops reading mastery, thereby fulfilling the unity of the whole language experience. The child is thus led to read, write, spell, speak, and listen more confidently.

Why Thematic Planning?

One very useful tool for implementing an integrated language program is thematic planning. By choosing a theme with a correlating literature selection for a unit of study, a teacher can plan activities throughout the day that lead to a cohesive, in-depth study of the topic. Children will be practicing and applying their skills in meaningful context. Consequently, they tend to learn and retain more.

Why Cooperative Learning?

Besides academic skills and content, children need to learn social skills. No longer can this area of development be taken for granted. Children must learn to work cooperatively in groups in order to function well in modern society. Group activities should be a regular part of school life and teachers should consciously include social objectives as well as academic objectives in their planning.

Why Big Books?

An excellent cooperative, whole language activity is the production of Big Books. Groups of children, or the whole class, can apply their language skills, content knowledge, and creativity to produce a big book that becomes a part of the classroom library to be read and reread. These books make excellent culminating projects for sharing beyond the classroom with parents, librarians, other classes, etc.

Why Journals?

Each day your children should have the opportunity to write in a journal. They may respond to a book or an event in history, write about a personal experience, or answer a general "question of the day" posed by the teacher. The cumulative journal provides an excellent means of documenting children's writing progress.

Stellaluna

by Janell Cannon

Summary

Stellaluna is the heartwarming story of a baby bat's desire to be reunited with her mother. Along the way she is adopted by a family of birds where she learns to eat, sleep, and fly like a bird. Stellaluna is finally reunited with her mother, but the friendship with her bird siblings remains as they learn to appreciate each other...differences and all.

The outline below is a suggested plan for using the various activities that are presented in this unit.

Sample Plan

Lesson I

- Find out how your children feel about bats (page 8).

- Read *Stellaluna*.

- Use the Puppet Props to act out the story (page 6, Enjoying the Book, #3).

- Introduce the Bat Cave (page 67).

- Complete a Daily Writing Activity (pages 24 and 25).

Lesson II

- Reread *Stellaluna*. Have the children retell the story using verbal sequencing.

- Pictorially sequence the story events (page 9).

- Complete Now That's Talent! (page 6, #5).

- Learn about nocturnal animals (page 7, #1).

- Create Bats at Sunset (page 54).

- Continue Daily Writing Activities.

Lesson III

- Review the story, focus on the illustrations and emphasize the friendly behaviors of Stellaluna and her bird siblings.

- Read other stories about friendship (page 6, #4).

- Complete Blind as a Bat (page 27).

- Learn about megabats and microbats (page 7, #2).

- Discover more facts about megabats (page 37).

- Make Tissue-tube Bats (page 52).

- Continue Daily Writing Activities.

Lesson IV

- Listen to poems about bats (page 7, #3).

- Write a poem using the bat outline (page 77).

- Complete Wingspan Measurement (page 7, #4).

- Continue Daily Writing Activities.

Lesson V

- Play the Going Batty! math game (page 7, #5).

- Find out where bats live (page 7, #6).

- Make Windsock Bats (page 53).

- Treat you children to Fruit Bat Delight (page 57).

Overview of Activities

Setting the Stage

1. To prepare yourself for teaching about bats, read the scientific information found on pages 18, 21, 36-40, 42-46, 48-51, 58-59, 63-64, and 78.

2. Set the tone in your room for the bats unit by setting up the Creatures of the Night bulletin board (page 66) and the Bat Cave (page 67).

3. Begin the unit by asking the children to think about bats. Ask them what they know about these animals. Using chart paper, draw a three-column KWL (Know, Want To Know, Learned) chart. Have the children dictate their thoughts; record their responses in the first two columns. The final column should be completed throughout the unit as the children learn new information about bats.

Enjoying the Book

1. Read the book *Stellaluna* to your children. Periodically stop and enjoy the illustrations. Predict what will happen next.

2. Ask the children to retell the story. Have each child draw a picture of his or her favorite part of the story.

3. Reproduce, color, cut out, and glue the props on page 10 to tagboard. If desired, laminate props for durability. Staple or glue a craft stick to the bottom of each shape. Use the props to retell the story. (You can also enlarge the props onto tagboard, color, laminate, and wear them, tied with a string around the neck, as a costume prop.)

4. Read the story to the children again. Ask them to tell you the ways that Stellaluna and the birds helped each other. Ask the children to think about the ways they can be helpful to their own family members and friends. Read other stories about friendship and do friendship-related activities (page 12).

5. Discuss the things that bats and birds each do well, such as bats having the ability to see while flying at night and birds being able to land upright on tree branches. Follow up the discussion by having the children complete the chart on page 11.

6. Using the basic bulletin-board background for Going Batty Over Poetry (page 65), have the children create their own storyboard for *Stellaluna*. In one section of the bulletin board (preferably towards the far left side) show Stellaluna and her mother being attacked by the owl. In the next section show Stellaluna falling into the birds' nest, and so on. If you'd like, you can have the children write a caption or statement for each section of the story's representation on sentence strips and attach the sentence strip to the bulletin board.

6

Overview of Activities *(cont.)*

Extending the Book

1. Teach your children about nocturnal animals and have them learn about the nocturnal behaviors of bats by completing page 42.

2. Share information about the two types of bats—megabats and microbats. Information about megabats and microbats can be found on page 36. Based on the shared information, ask the children to determine whether Stellaluna is a megabat or a microbat.

3. Share the bat poems on page 23. Have the children create their own bat poems and write edited versions on the reproduced bat pattern (page 77). Display the children's poetry on the Going Batty Over Poetry bulletin board (page 65).

4. Bats come in all different sizes. Use the Wingspan Measurement activity (page 34) to illustrate to the children the variations of bats' wings and body sizes. If desired, duplicate the bat rulers on page 76 for the children's use.

5. To prepare the Going Batty! game, duplicate the gameboard, cards, and manipulative bats (pages 30, 31, and 32). Glue the gameboard to a sheet of tagboard; laminate for durability. (If desired, use the bat wing pattern on page 72 to trace two wings onto black construction paper. Glue the wing tabs under the edges of the two longer sides of the gameboard. The wings can be folded over the gameboard for storage.) Cut apart the game cards and manipulatives bats. On the back of each of the game cards randomly write a numeral 1 or 2. Place the game cards in a stack. While playing the game and completing the game card math problems, encourage the children to check their answers by using the manipulative bats.

6. Find out where in the world bats live. Duplicate and enlarge onto bulletin-board paper the map found on page 47. Display the map and discuss the locations of bats throughout the world. Explain that bats live in all parts of the world except for Antarctica. Fruit bats, like Stellaluna, live in Africa, Asia, and Australia. Have the children complete copies of pages 46 and 47. As the children learn about new bats, attach labels (or use reproduced bat patterns, page 54) to the map to show the bats' home locations, as well as add the newly-discovered information to the third column of your KWL chart (page 6, Setting the Stage, #3).

7. Enjoy a sweet tasting bat treat by creating one of the Batty Edibles (page 57).

8. Encourage the children to memorize some or all of the bat songs (page 55). If they can sing them to you, award them with a batty badge (page 68).

9. If you are Internet-accessible, have the children explore the world of bat facts via some of the Web sites listed on pages 58 and 59.

Do You Like Bats?

Before reading the story *Stellaluna,* ask the children to think about how they feel about bats. Create a three-column opinion graph "cave" using brown bulletin-board paper as illustrated below. The middle columns and bat-cave edges are formed using rolled-up sections of the brown bulletin-board paper.

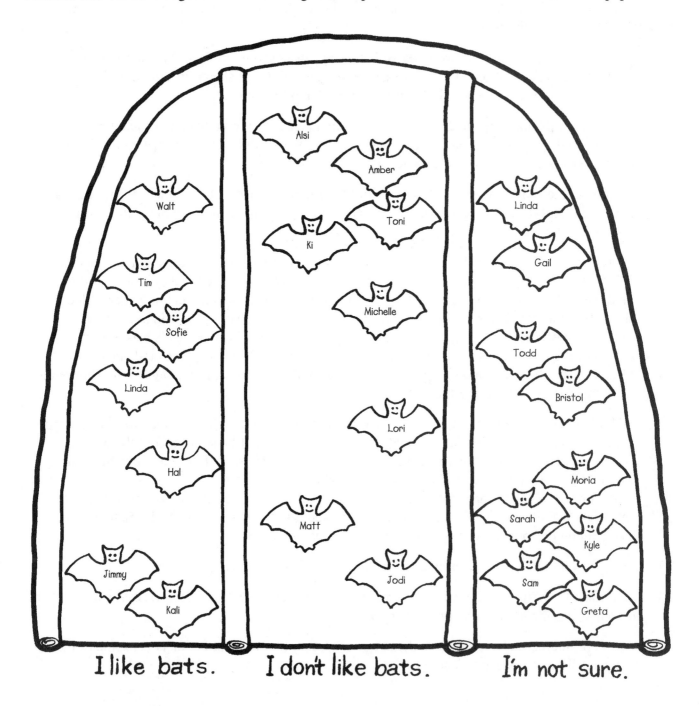

Provide each child with a reproduced bat pattern (page 77). Have each child color and cut out the bat and write his/her name on the front of the bat. Each child then places his or her bat on the graph by taping or stapling the bat in the appropriate column describing how he or she presently feels about bats. At the end of the bat unit look again at the bat cave and allow the children to move their bats to show how they now feel about bats.

Story Sequencing

Read the six sentences. Cut apart the six illustrations and glue them onto a new piece of paper in the correct story order.

Stellaluna fell into a bird nest.

Stellaluna found her mother.

Stellaluna protected and saved her bird friends.

Mother bird fed Stellaluna.

Stellaluna and the baby birds learned to fly.

Mother and Stellaluna were attacked by an owl.

Puppet Props

See page 6, #3 for suggested use.

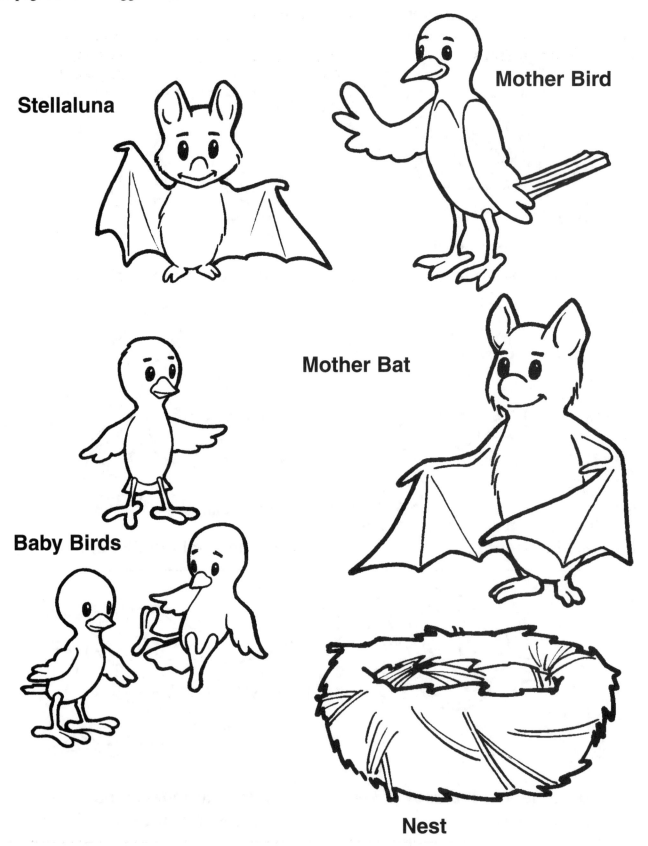

Stellaluna

Mother Bird

Mother Bat

Baby Birds

Nest

Now That's Talent!

Bats and birds each have their own talents. You have talents, too. Complete the chart below by writing your thoughts or drawing pictures.

Things Bats Do Well	Things Birds Do Well	Things I Do Well

Friends Helping Friends

Stellaluna and her bird siblings are special friends. They were able to help one another in times of trouble. Share other stories of friendship. Here are two to get you started:

The Island of the Skog by Steven Kellogg

A group of mice travel to a distant island to find a peaceful new home. They soon learn that the island is home to a skog, but they don't know what a skog is. This story shows how setting aside our fears and working together can bring about true friendship.

Activities

1. After reading *The Island of the Skog*, have the children tell about the friendships they noticed throughout the story. Which characters treated others with kindness? Which characters were bossy?

2. Have the children brainstorm behaviors they can exhibit to develop friendships with others. Record their responses on chart paper.

3. Review the list of brainstormed friendship behaviors each day and encourage your children to use these behaviors to treat each other with kindness and respect.

Frog and Toad are Friends by Arnold Lobel

Frog and Toad have a friendship that endures through good times and bad. This book has five different chapter-like stories about friends helping friends.

Activities

1. After reading *The Story*, ask the children to tell what they would do to cheer up a friend who wasn't feeling well. Ask the children to write stories about times when they have helped their friends or actually have them make small gifts to give to friends or classmates who need encouragement.

2. Read *The Letter*. Ask the children to tell you how they feel when they receive letters in the mail. In the story, Toad feels sad that he never receives mail. Frog decides to mail a letter to his friend to cheer him up. Invite each child to write a letter and/or draw a picture to be sent or given to a friend or family member.

3. Ask the children to think about someone that is a good friend. Ask them to think about their favorite activity that they like doing with that friend. Have the children write individual short stories about enjoying the activities they do with their good friends. Have them also illustrate their stories.

12

Zipping, Zapping, Zooming Bats

by Ann Earle

Summary

This beautifully illustrated book provides a vast array of factual information presented in an understandable manner. Your children will learn about bats' body structure, food eaten, echolocation, where bats live, and much, much more.

The outline below is a suggested plan for using the various activities that are presented in this unit.

Sample Plan

Lesson I

- Complete Pal or Pest? (page 17).
- Read *Zipping, Zapping, Zooming Bats.*
- Learn about Bat Anatomy (page 14, Enjoying the Book, #2).
- Share Microbat Facts information (page 38).
- Sing the bat songs (page 55).
- Write bat songs (page 56).
- Visit bat Web sites (pages 58 and 59).

Lesson II

- Complete the Bat Vocabulary activity (page 14, Enjoying the Book, #3).
- Review *Zipping, Zapping, Zooming Bats.*
- Learn about sound waves and echolocation (page 15, #4).
- Solve a couple of the critical thinking questions (page 14, Extending the Book, #1).
- Sing some of the child-created bat songs from Lesson l.
- Begin bat research (page 15, #5).

Lesson III

- Identify and write bat facts and opinions (pages 28 and 29).
- Conduct Favorite Bat Surveys (page 15, #6).
- Guess the names of bats with strange noses (page 15, #7).
- Revisit the bat Web sites (pages 58 and 59).
- Go on a Web site scavenger hunt (page 15, #9).

Lesson IV

- Learn about Carlsbad Caverns (page 15, #10).
- Learn about baby bats and their mothers (page 43).
- Learn about bat guano (page 45).
- Make big books about bats (page 15, #8).
- Enjoy a tasty bat treat (page 57).

Lesson V

- Learn about endangered bats (page 50).
- Share ideas of how to protect endangered bats (page 15, #11).
- Play You're up to Bat! (page 16, #14).
- Enjoy the culminating bat activities (page 61).

Overview of Activities

Setting the Stage

---

1. If you have not already done so, complete Do You Like Bats? (page 8).

2. Before reading the book, have the children discuss their perceptions of bats. Some things people believe about bats are merely myths. Have the children read along with you as you read a transparency, placed on an overhead projector, that you have made of page 21. Be certain to discuss the difference in meaning between a myth and a fact.

Enjoying the Book

---

1. Reread the book *Zipping, Zapping, Zooming Bats*. Invite the children to share facts that they found interesting in the book. Add the learned facts to your KWL chart (page 6, Setting the Stage, #3). Encourage the children to ask you questions to help clarify concepts they do not yet comprehend.

2. Complete the bat anatomy activities on page 18 and then have your children work in small groups or individually to complete page 19.

3. Introduce and define the vocabulary words using the word bank at the bottom of page 26. After discussing each word, distribute copies of page 26 to the children and have them solve the vocabulary crossword puzzle on their own or as a total group.

echolocation   *colony*   *mammal*   *roost*

Extending the Book

---

1. The critical thinking questions on page 35 will challenge your children to use their mathematical brainpower while also learning more interesting facts about bats. Pose one or two questions a day.

2. Duplicate page 20 for your children. Have them list three bats of their choice in the first column and research their three choices. To complete the bat chart, have the children use literature resources (Bibliography, page 79) or the Internet (Web sites, pages 58 and 59).

3. Teach your children the bat songs on page 55. Distribute copies of page 56 and have the children fill in the blanks to create their own bat songs.

Overview of Activities *(cont.)*

Extending the Book *(cont.)*

4. Your children will be fascinated to learn how sound waves travel and how bats use sound waves to catch insects and other small creatures. Share the sound wave and echolocation information and complete the activities found on pages 39 and 40.

5. Distribute copies of the research sheet on page 22. Ask each child to choose a bat that he or she would like to learn more about. Provide bat resource books, encyclopedias, and Internet Web sites for the children to use to complete the questions (Bibliography, page 79). When the children have completed their research, have them use their gained information to write and/or orally present short reports.

6. Using the Graph Your Bat Survey provides a fun way for children to practice surveying and graphing skills. Provide each child with a copy of page 33. Have each child write the names of four different bats on the chart. Have each child then survey classmates (in your room or in another class) to determine which bat seems to be the favorite. Display the results and make mathematical comparisons.

7. Explain to the children that many microbats have unusual noses. Scientists believe that microbats use their noses to direct sounds waves for echolocation. Many of these bats are named after their noses. Have each child complete page 41, matching the names of the bats to their images.

8. Have the children display their bat knowledge by creating big books. See page 73 for step-by-step directions for making big books.

9. After allowing the children to investigate bat Web sites (pages 58 and 59), provide each child with a copy of the scavenger hunt for the Bat Conservation International site (page 60). The children will need to investigate the Web site in order to complete the scavenger hunt.

10. Carlsbad Caverns is not only home to bats, but also to many interesting formations. Have the children view photographs of the inside of the cavern by accessing the Carlsbad Caverns Web site (page 59) and encouraging them to record the information discovered about the cavern and the bats that live there.

11. Inspire the children to make a difference in the world of bats. Use the ideas on page 51 to help save bats and spread the word to others.

12. Have the children display their knowledge of bats on a bulletin board entitled Not So Batty Facts (page 65).

Overview of Activities *(cont.)*

Extending the Book *(cont.)*

13. If bats live in your area, your children may want to attract bats to their backyards by making bat houses. Assemble copies of the bat house instruction booklet on pages 62-64 to use during the building process. If bats do not live in your area, consider making a bat house to donate to the Bat Conservation International, P.O. Box 162603, Austin, TX 78716.

14. Children will enjoy testing their bat I.Q. by playing You're up to Bat! Duplicate a copy of the gameboard (page 70); laminate for durability. (If desired, use the bat wing pattern on page 72 to trace two wings onto black construction paper. Glue the wing tabs under the edges of the two longer sides of the gameboard. The wings can be folded over the gameboard for storage.) Duplicate the question cards (pages 69 and 71) back-to-back; cut apart the cards. (The questions will be on one side and the answers on the other side.)

The children play the game in groups of two or three. To begin, the first player is asked a question from the question card stack. If answered correctly, he or she earns 10 points. The question card is then placed atop one of the 10-point spaces on the gameboard and that child awards him or herself 10 points on a tally sheet. When all 10-point spaces are covered, the questions now become worth 20 points and so on. Play continues, in turn, until all questions have been answered. Players then tally up their total points (no points for incorrect answers) to declare a winner.

Note: This game can also be played wherein the question cards are made up by the children based on bat facts they have learned throughout the unit.

Pal or Pest?

Read the information below. Fill in the blanks.

Do you think bats are pals or pests?

Many people fear them, but they are really very helpful. If there were no bats, there would be too many insects. Did you know that a Little Brown bat can eat 150 bugs in 15 minutes or 600 tiny mosquitoes in one hour!

Bats are very helpful to farmers. Hungry, plant-eating bugs can quickly destroy the farmers' crops. Bats eat grasshoppers, beetles, and moths. Farmers like bats "hanging around" their crop fields.

1. How do bugs kill plants?

   _____

2. How are bats helpful to farmers?

   _____

3. What kinds of bugs do bats eat?

   _____

4. How many bugs can a Little Brown bat eat in one hour?

   _____

5. Do you think a bat is a pal or a pest? Why?

   _____

Draw your favorite bat on the back of this paper.

Bat Anatomy Facts

Wings

Bats are the only mammals that have wings. Even though they can fly, their wings and bodies are very different from birds. Bats actually have legs, arms, and fingers. The wings just make their body parts difficult to recognize. The arms and fingers of bats are what give structure to the wing membrane so bats can fly. The wing membrane is made of strong skin that is stretched tightly over the fingers. Like a human, bats have a thumb and four fingers on each hand. Bats' wings are like webbed hands. Bats can maneuver their wings or tail to catch a bug and toss it into their mouths. Bats can move their wings in ways a bird cannot. Bats' wings are extremely large compared to the sizes of their bodies. They have strong shoulder muscles that are used to move the wings and help make them great fliers. Some bats fly very slowly which allows them to change directions quickly. There are even some kinds of bats that can hover in place like helicopters.

Claws

Bats' small feet are attached to the lower portion of the wings. Bats have claws on their feet and one claw on each thumb. They use these claws to hang upside down, clean their fur and ears, and move around in their roosts.

Fur

Bats do not have feathers on their bodies. They are covered with fur. While their wings appear to be bare they are actually covered with tiny hairs.

Activities

1. Share the above information with your children. Show pictures or photographs of different types of bats (Bibliography, page 79). Encourage the children to try and identify the bats' legs, claws, wing and tail membranes, arms, fingers, thumbs, and fur.

2. Duplicate page 19 for each child. To complete the page, the child labels the parts of the bat by cutting and pasting the words in the correct places.

Bat Anatomy

A bat has many body parts. Cut out each word box below and paste it next to the matching part of the bats body.

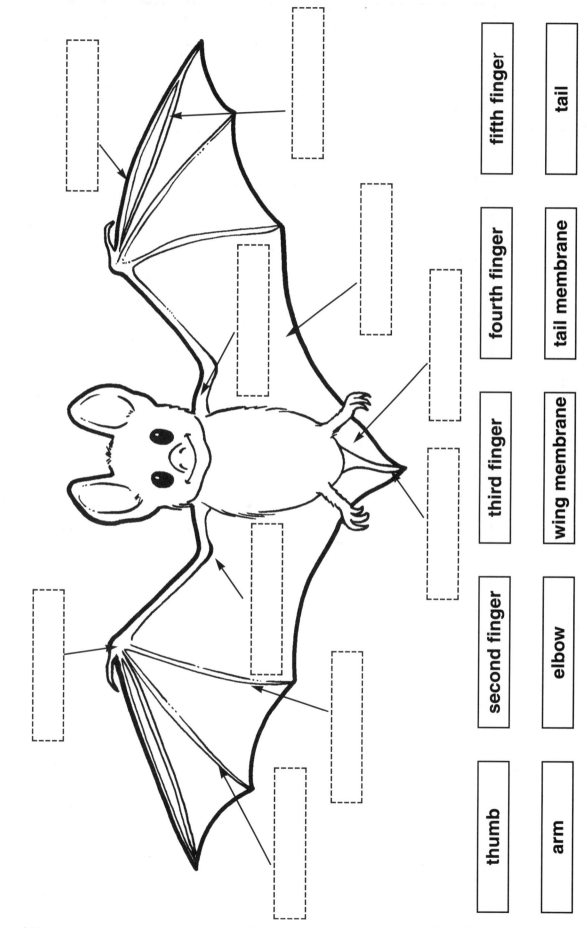

fifth finger

tail

fourth finger

tail membrane

third finger

wing membrane

second finger

elbow

thumb

arm

Bat Chart

Bat Name	What it Eats	Where it Lives	Interesting Facts

Do You Believe That Myth?

A myth is something that many people believe that really is not true.

Myth 1

Some people believe that bats attack people.

Bats are really very shy animals. They are gentle and helpful. Some bats help to pollinate plants. Some bats eat harmful bugs.

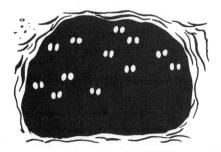

Myth 2

Some people believe bats are blind.

That is not true. All bats can see. Some bats do not use their eyes to catch bugs. They use echolocation. Many bats have very good eyesight. They have large eyes and can see well in the dark.

Myth 3

Some people believe that bats have rabies.

Rabies is a dangerous disease. All animals can get rabies, but most bats do not have rabies.

Myth 4

Some people believe that bats nest in peoples' hair.

Bats live in trees, caves, and other safe places. They are wild animals and are naturally afraid of people.

Bat Research

Choose one bat to study. Answer the questions below.

What is the name of your bat?_____

Is it a megabat or microbat? _____

What does it eat? _____

How does the bat find its food? _____

_____

_____

Where does the bat live? _____

_____

Does the bat hibernate? _____

_____

What interesting facts have you learned about your bat?

_____

_____

_____

_____

_____

Use the information above to help you write a research report. Draw a picture to go along with your report.

Batty Poems

Those Bats

They come in many colors,

Flying through the nighttime air.

They use sonar to guide their way,

Those bats are everywhere!

They eat so many little bugs,

The farmers love them so.

But when the daylight comes along,

Do you know where they go?

Bats

Flying, flying in the sky,

Bats are neat, I'll tell you why.

Flying foxes are the tallest,

Bumblebee bats are the smallest.

Bats are yellow, red, and brown,

Bats sleep hanging upside-down.

Some eat bugs and some eat fruit,

Some look mean and some look cute.

Flying, flying in the sky,

Bats are neat, now you know why!

Amazing Bats

Amazing bats like to eat—

Thousands of bugs for a tasty treat.

Flying through the moonlit air—

Traveling here and traveling there.

Hibernating when the weather's cold—

Gathered with hundreds of friends, I'm told.

Many bats are endangered, I'm sad to say—

There are fewer and fewer bats every day.

Be kind to bats, that's the thing to do—

Tell your friends and your family, too!

Daily Writing Activities

Bat Riddles

Your children can create amusing riddles about different bats they have researched. To write a riddle, each child chooses one bat and identifies two or three characteristics to use in writing the riddle. Here is an example:

**I have small eyes.
I use echolocation to hunt.
My nose has a flap shaped like a leaf.
What am I?**

(Answer: A leaf-nosed bat.)

Accordion Book

An accordion book is a wonderful way for the children to display their knowledge of bats. To make the book, cut one white and one colored strip of stiff paper each 6" x 36" (15cm x 91cm). Position the colored strip horizontally on a tabletop and squeeze a trail of glue along the top 36" (91 cm) edge. Affix the white strip to the colored strip by overlapping the edges of the two strips. When the glue is dry, accordion-fold the paper into six vertical panel sections (each panel will be 6" x 12" [15cm x 30cm]). The first panel of the book is for the cover illustration (top section) and the book's title (bottom section). On each remaining panel, the child writes an interesting bat fact on the lower half of the panel and an illustration on the upper half.

How Would You Feel?

Stellaluna was separated from her mother when she was just a baby. Ask children how they think she felt. Then have them write about how they would feel if they were separated from their families, as well as how they would feel once reunited.

24

Daily Writing Activities *(cont.)*

Journal Thoughts

To inspire children's journal writing, display one of the following questions daily:

- *Would you rather be a bird or a bat? Why?*

- *What do you think it would be like to live in a cave?*

- *Imagine that you had to sleep upside down. What do you think that would be like?*

- *Would you rather be a megabat or a microbat? Why?*

- *If you could see in the dark, what would you do?*

Adjective Web

Enhance children's writing by having them work in pairs or individually to complete an adjective web. The web is begun by writing the word *bats* in a circle (or in a bat shape) in the center of a sheet of paper. The children then add extending lines from the center circle and write adjectives that describe bats.

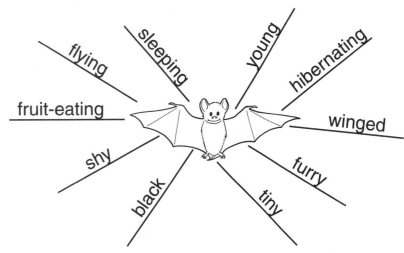

Draw and Write

- *Draw* a picture of Stellaluna with the baby birds. *Write* about the things they did together.

- *Draw* a picture of yourself as a bat. *Write* about what it would be like to be a bat for a day.

- Stellaluna and the baby birds helped each other in many ways. *Draw* a picture of a time when you were helpful and *write* about it.

Sharing Time

Invite your children to share their writings with one another. Divide them into small groups of three or four. Ask each child to choose one piece of writing to bring to a sharing group. The children take turns reading their stories, poems, riddles, or other writings. Encourage the groups to ask each other questions or comment on what has been shared.

Bat Vocabulary

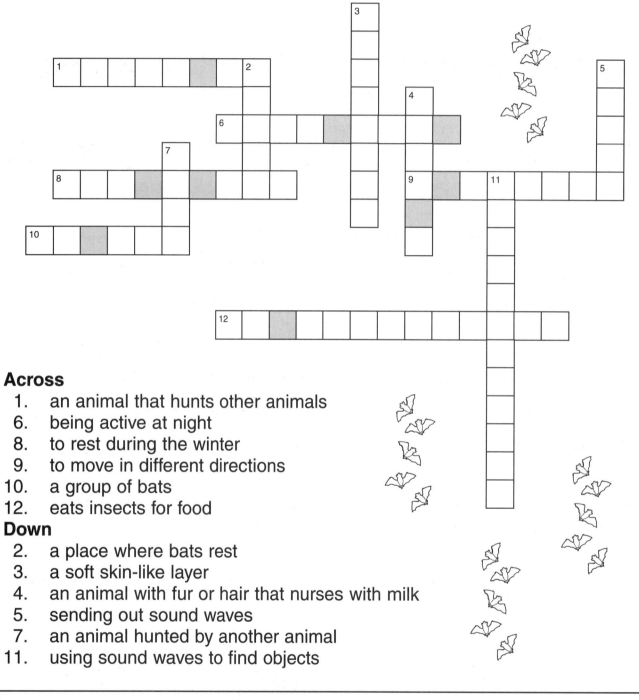

Across
1. an animal that hunts other animals
6. being active at night
8. to rest during the winter
9. to move in different directions
10. a group of bats
12. eats insects for food

Down
2. a place where bats rest
3. a soft skin-like layer
4. an animal with fur or hair that nurses with milk
5. sending out sound waves
7. an animal hunted by another animal
11. using sound waves to find objects

Word Bank

echolocation	roost	predator	insectivorous
membrane	hibernate	prey	maneuver
mammal	colony	nocturnal	sonar

A Batty Bonus Idea: Make a bat word using all of the letters in the shaded boxes (you will need to unscramble the letters to make the word).

Blind as a Bat

Bats are not blind. In fact, some have very good eyesight. The saying, *blind as a bat*, is a simile.

A simile compares two different things using the word *like* or *as.*

Read the list of similes below. Write T (true), F (false) or T/F (true and false) beside each one. Talk to a friend about why you made the answer choices you did.

1. blind as a bat _____   2. thick as a brick _____

3. hard as a rock _____   4. high as a mountain_____

5. sweet as candy _____   6. sly as a fox _____

7. sharp as a tack _____   8. quick as a whip_____

9. cute as a button _____   10. pleased as punch _____

11. bright as the sun _____   12. quiet as a mouse _____

13. tall as a tree _____   14. white as a sheet _____

Try to think of two new similes. Write them on the lines below. Don't forget to use the word *like* or *as.*

_____

_____

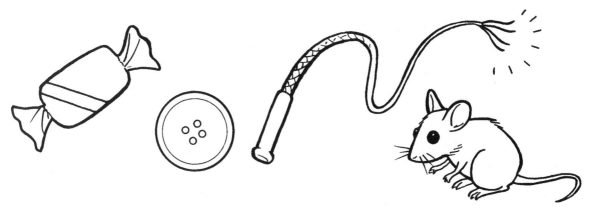

Fact vs. Opinion

A *fact* is something that is true.
Bats can fly.

An *opinion* tells the way someone feels about something.
Bats are fun to watch.

Read the sentences below. Write *fact* or *opinion* beside each sentence. Talk to a friend about why you made the answer choices you did.

1. Flying foxes are large bats. _____

2. Vampire bats are scary. _____

3. Most bats hibernate. _____

4. Some bats catch fish. _____

5. Bumblebee bats are cute. _____

6. Leaf-nosed bats are cool. _____

7. The Carlsbad Caverns are pretty. _____

8. Many bats live in caves. _____

9. It would be fun to see in the dark. _____

10. Bats are nocturnal. _____

11. Bats have fingers and thumbs. _____

12. Bats are ugly. _____

13. Bats are the best kind of mammal. _____

14. There are many kinds of bats. _____

28

Bat Fact and Opinion Chart

Write one fact and one opinion sentence about bats. Illustrate each sentence.

My Fact Sentence	My Opinion Sentence

Going Batty! Gameboard

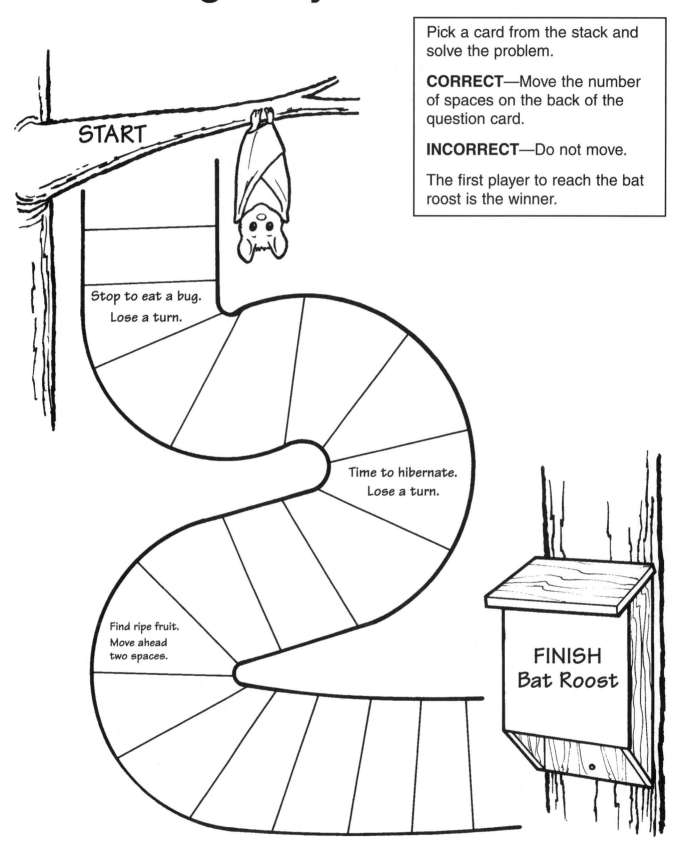

Pick a card from the stack and solve the problem.

CORRECT—Move the number of spaces on the back of the question card.

INCORRECT—Do not move.

The first player to reach the bat roost is the winner.

START

Stop to eat a bug.
Lose a turn.

Time to hibernate.
Lose a turn.

Find ripe fruit.
Move ahead
two spaces.

FINISH
Bat Roost

Going Batty! Game Cards

13 fruit bats in a tree. 5 fly away. How many bats are left?	7 red bats. 5 gray bats. How many more red bats?
7 gray bats in the cave. 7 gray bats outside. How many bats in all?	10 flying foxes. 3 vampire bats. How many more flying foxes?
12 vampire bats in a roost. 3 go to sleep. How many bats are awake?	16 fruit bats. 9 found fruit to eat. How many did not find fruit to eat?
18 megabats clean their fur. 7 megabats are still sleeping. How many bats in all?	15 megabats. 8 microbats. How many bats in all?
14 microbats are hunting. 6 fly back to the cave. How many microbats are left?	5 bats clean their fur. 6 bats clean their ears. How many bats in all?
4 flying foxes like nectar. 6 flying foxes like fruit. How many flying foxes in all?	19 bats in a cave. 6 leave to hunt. How many bats are left?
8 bats are gray. 4 bats are brown. 3 bats are white. How many bats in all?	4 butterfly bats. 7 ghost bats. 6 red bats. How many bats in all?
11 bat pups are in a cave. 6 fly away. How many pups are left?	12 bats in a cave. 7 are sleeping. How many are not sleeping?
17 bats sleeping in a tree. 10 bats sleeping in a cave. How many bats in all?	3 bats roost in a barn. 8 bats roost in a tree. How many bats in all?

Going Batty! Manipulatives

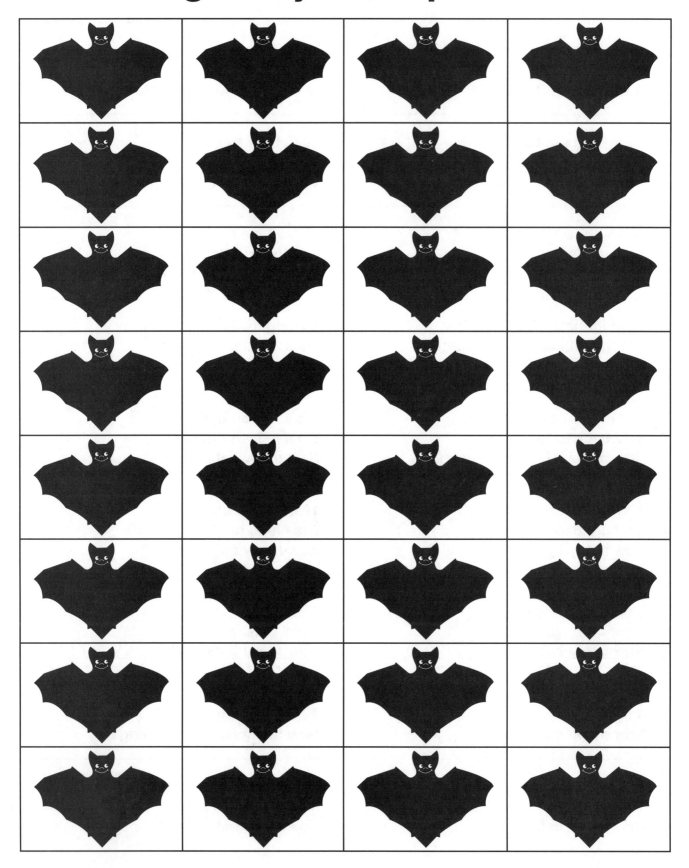

Graph Your Bat Survey

Write the name of a different bat next to each letter on the graph. Conduct a survey to find out people's favorite bat. Color one square for each person's favorite bat.

A								
B								
C								
D								
	1st person	2nd person	3rd person	4th person	5th person	6th person	7th person	8th person
Bat's Name								

Use your completed graph to answer the following questions.

1. Which bat did the people like the best?

_____

2. Which bat did the people like the least?

_____

3. What did you learn from this survey?

_____

Wingspan Measurement

Bats come in many different sizes. For each bat listed below, find something in your room that is the same size and write the name of that item on the line.

1. The body of a **yellow-winged bat** is **14 centimeters**.

_____

2. The body of a **fruit bat** is **16 inches**.

_____

3. The body of a **vampire bat** is **3 ½ inches**.

_____

4. The wingspan of a **hog-nosed bat** is **5 inches**.

_____

5. The body of a **hog-nosed bat** is **1 ½ inches**.

_____

6. The body of the **big brown bat** is **4 inches** long.

_____

7. The wingspan of a **big brown bat** is about **12 inches**.

_____

8. The body of a **bent-wing bat** is about **6 centimeters**.

_____

9. The wingspan of a **bent-wing bat** is **9 centimeters**.

_____

10. The wingspan of a **flying fox bat** is about **6 feet**!

_____

Critical Thinking Challenge

Below is a list of questions to encourage mathematical thinking. Pose one or two questions a day. Provide scrap paper or journal entry paper so that the children can show their logic via illustration or mathematical computation.

1. In Carlsbad Caverns, three hundred bats sometimes gather in a one-foot square space. How many bats would fit in a two-foot square? A five-foot square?

2. If the wingspan of a microbat is five inches, how many bats would it take to equal 15 inches?

3. A bat has five fingers at the end of each wing. How many fingers does it have altogether? If you count the fingers on eight bats, how many fingers would there be in all?

4. The inside temperature of Carlsbad Caverns is 56 degrees Fahrenheit (14 degrees Celsius). If the temperature outside the cave is 78 degrees Fahrenheit (26 degrees Celsius), how much hotter is it outside than inside?

5. A brown bat can catch 150 insects in 15 minutes. How many insects can it catch in 30 minutes?

6. There are about 1,000 different kinds of bats. If 800 of them are microbats, how many of them are megabats?

7. Some bats have two babies each year. How many babies would a mother bat have after seven years if she had two babies each year?

8. The largest bat is the flying fox. Its body is about 16 inches (48 cm) long. How many inches (centimeters) longer than one foot (30cm) is the flying fox?

9. Some bats can fly as fast as 60 miles per hour. At this speed, how many miles could a bat travel in three hours?

10. A bat can live to be 30 years old. How old is the bat when it has lived half of its life?

Megabats and Microbats

Scientists divide bats into two groups—megabats and microbats. There are about 200 kinds of megabats and about 800 kinds of microbats.

Megabats have large eyes and excellent eyesight. Most megabats have short, round ears. Most megabats eat fruit and have a good sense of smell so that they can find ripened fruit. They can have wingspans up to six feet (1.90 meters). They roost together in trees and wrap their wings around themselves to keep warm.

Microbats are generally smaller than megabats with wingspans up to five inches (13cm). They have large ears and small eyes. Most microbats eat insects and use echolocation to hunt. Their ears and noses come in a variety of shapes and sizes.

Activities

1. Share the above information with your children. As your children research bats, ask them to identify whether the bats are megabats or microbats. Encourage them to look at the size of the bats' eyes and ears, wingspans, and the kinds of foods eaten in order to help them arrive at their conclusions.

2. Display two sheets of chart paper—one labeled Megabats, the other labeled Microbats. As the children identify and learn about different bats, write the names of the bats on the chart under the appropriate heading.

3. Ask the children to determine whether Stellaluna is a megabat or a microbat. What characteristics helped them to determine this?

4. Have each child choose one type of bat to illustrate. Below the illustration have the child write the name of the bat (Example: Flying Fox), it's group name (Example: Megabat), and some characteristics of that particular bat that helps in classifying it either as a megabat or a microbat.

5. Conduct research to find out if bats live in your part of the world (Web sites, pages 58 and 59, and Bibliography, page 79, may prove helpful). Determine if the bats that live in your area are megabats, microbats, or both.

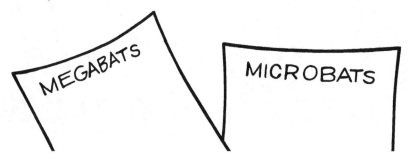

Megabat Facts

Most megabats carry their babies when they fly.

Megabats are the largest bats.

Megabats like to roost in trees.

The largest megabat's wingspan is six feet.

Most megabats eat fruit or flowers' nectar.

Megabats do not use echolocation. They have great eyesight.

Microbat Facts

All microbats use echolocation to find their food.

Some microbats hunt for fish using echolocation.

Most microbats live only in the Western Hemisphere.

Most microbats are small enough to fit in your hand.

Some microbat colonies have 20 million bats.

The smallest microbat weighs less than a penny.

38

Making Waves

Sound Waves

Sound is produced by sound waves that pass through the air to your ear. Every sound begins from a vibrating source. Show your children how sound waves travel by completing the following demonstration:

Fill a small, plastic wading pool halfway with water. Gather the children in a large circle around the wading pool. Explain to the children that sound waves move through the air in much the same way that waves travel through water. As the children observe, gently tap the water on one outer side of the pool. Ask the children to watch how the waves move across the pool (it will appear as a ripple). Explain that when someone speaks vibrations travel through the air in the same way. (Note: This principle can also be demonstrated in smaller groups gathered around a small plastic tub of water.)

Sound Knowledge

Tell the children that the outer portion of our ears help to catch sound waves. The larger the ear the more sound waves can be caught. Display pictures of bats with large ears (microbats). Ask the children to compare the ears of the bats to the size of the bats' bodies. Ask questions such as, "Why do you think these bats have such large ears?" Then ask, "Do you think a bat's hearing is better or worse than yours?" Have the children cup their hands around their ears. Continue speaking to them and ask them to tell you what they notice. If desired, extend this activity by having each child create an even larger "ear" by cupping a sheet of paper around his or her ears. What happens now to the sounds they hear?

Pitch It To Me

Sounds can have a low pitch or a high pitch. Sometimes sounds cannot be heard by the human ear. When sound waves vibrate slowly, a low-pitched sound is produced. When sound waves vibrate quickly, a high-pitched sound is produced. Provide each child, or pair of children, with a shoebox (shoebox lid is not needed) and different sizes and thicknesses of rubberbands. The children are to stretch several different sizes of rubberbands around the entire shoebox's girth. The children then pluck each rubberband and observe the visual vibrations. Do some rubberbands seem to vibrate faster than others? (thinner vs. thicker bands) What is the difference in the pitch (sound) of each rubberband? (low or high) Do tighter rubberbands make different sounds than looser ones?

Echolocation

Echolocation is the method that some bats use to catch insects and other moving creatures. They are able to use sound waves to determine where the insect is. When a bat is hunting it makes a series of high-pitched sounds. The sound waves travel through the air and bounce off of objects. When the sound waves return to the bat it can tell the bat where the object is. A bat can use sound waves to tell the difference between objects that are stationary or moving. For example, a bat uses sound waves to avoid hitting a tree and immediately afterwards uses sound waves to catch a mosquito. Bats probably have the best techniques for echolocation of any animal on earth. The sounds they make are often much higher than the human ear can hear.

How do sound waves travel back to a bat? It is similar to how a mirror reflects light. If you hold a small mirror in your hand and maneuver it in the sunlight you can see the light reflecting off of the mirror and onto other objects. This is similar to how sound waves are reflected. The bat emits a high-frequency sound. The sound waves hit an object and are then reflected back to the bat. This high-tech system allows bats to fly in total darkness. They not only "see" where they are going, but can also catch their prey. When you look at pictures of bats you can see that many have large ears and interesting nose shapes. Some bats use their ears to catch sound waves and other bats use their odd-shaped noses to direct sound waves.

Activities

1. Provide your children with hand mirrors and take them outside on a sunny day. Ask each child to reflect the sunlight off of the mirror and onto the sidewalk, side of a wall, or the school building. Ask the child to think about how the mirror is reflecting the light. Explain that bats reflect sound waves off of objects in much the same way. (**Note:** Warn the children to not reflect the light directly back towards their open eyes.)

2. Gather the children around you and ask them to look at the size of their classmates' ears in comparison to their bodies. Show pictures of bats with large ears and ask the children to compare the size of the ears to the bats' bodies. Remind the children that megabats have small ears and microbats have large ears (page 36). Are humans more like megabats or microbats? Have the children cup their hands around their ears. Continue talking to the children and ask if they notice a difference in the loudness of your voice. Ask them to tell why they think the sound is louder. Provide each child with a large circle (with approximately a 12" [30cm] diameter) that has been cut in half. Ask the children to cup one half-circle paper around each ear to form a pair of larger ears. Talk to the children for a few minutes with their larger ears in place. Be certain to not talk louder than when the children initially listened to your voice. Ask them to share how you sounded to them this time. Did your voice sound louder? Explain to children that their enlarged ears were able to collect more sound waves which improves their hearing.

What a Nose!

Many bats have noses that look odd. Cut out the bat names and glue the names in the correct boxes.

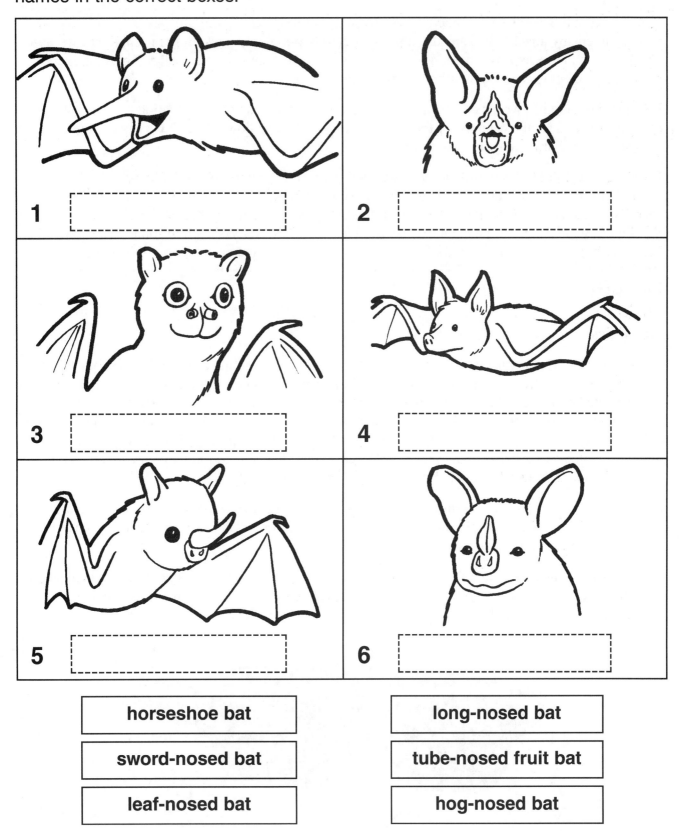

horseshoe bat	long-nosed bat
sword-nosed bat	tube-nosed fruit bat
leaf-nosed bat	hog-nosed bat

Creatures of the Night

Nocturnal animals are creatures that are most active at night. Bats are nocturnal. Their bodies are specialized so they can fly and hunt in the dark.

Being nocturnal benefits bats in many ways. Resting in safe places during the day helps to protect them from enemy attack. Bats are also able keep their bodies cool by avoiding the sunlight. Because bats have such large expanses of skin for their body size, they can overheat easily. Roosting in cool places helps them to regulate their body temperature.

Being nocturnal also give bats an advantage in hunting. Most bats use echolocation (see page 40) to catch insects and small creatures for food. The nighttime hours allow bats to hunt without the competition of diurnal (daytime) animals.

During the daylight hours, most bats congregate in caves, trees, or corners of buildings. At dusk, bats begin to awaken. At this time they begin their cleaning rituals. Bats are very clean animals and they spend time each evening combing their fur and cleaning their ears using their tongues and claws. When the sun has gone down for the night bats begin to leave their roosts in search of food. When daylight approaches they fly back to their homes. When approaching the bat cave or other living quarters many bats fly high over the opening of the roost, tuck their wings near their bodies, and dive with great speed into their home.

Activities

1. Ask the children what they could do to help them to move around a dark room without bumping into things. Divide the children into groups of two. Have one child blindfold the other. Have the sighted child guide his or her partner around the room by gently holding arms or shoulders and giving verbal directions. Have the children switch roles and move around the room in the same manner. In a large setting group, ask the children to discuss this experience. Ask them if they used other senses since they were blindfolded. Were they able to use their ears to tell where other children were? How did the experience make them feel?

2. If you haven't already, discuss the information about sound waves and echolocation on pages 39 and 40. Encourage the children to discuss bats' unique qualities that make them equipped for flying, maneuvering, and seeing in the dark.

3. If you are fortunate enough to see a show dedicated to bats on a learning television channel, record the show so that you can share it with your children. Many learning-channel bat specials feature bats leaving their cave at dusk for their evening feeding.

Shh! The Baby's Sleeping

Mammals are animals that have fur or hair on their bodies and who deliver via live birth rather than having their offspring hatch from eggs. Mammal mothers produce milk to nourish their babies. Bats are the only flying animals that nurse their babies with mothers' milk. When the babies are very young, the mother bats carry them, clinging to the bodies, as they hunt. Later, the babies are left in a portion of the cave home called the nursery. A mother returns, at least twice each night, to feed her baby called a pup. Nurseries can have hundreds of pups hanging together upside down, yet amazingly, a mother is able to find her own baby by its smell and the sounds of its cries! The bat pups, born in the spring, usually take their first flight when they are a month old. Soon after that they fly outside the cave and find their own food. By the fall, young bats are able to fly along with the adults to warmer climates.

Activities

1. Discuss with your children the difference between mammals and other types of animals. Based on the information given above, have the children determine whether or not dogs, cats, turtles, birds, and fish are mammals.

2. Ask the children to think about the care a mother bat gives her baby. Does the mother leave her baby alone? How long does the mother care for her baby before it can fly? Ask the children to think about the length of time human mothers care for their babies. How does this differ from bats? Discuss their responses.

3. Ask the children to create illustrations showing the similarities between bats and humans. To complete this project, give each child a sheet of paper. Have each child fold the paper in half, creating two sections. On one half of the page, the child draws a bat illustration and on the opposite half, an illustration of a human. For example, a child might draw a picture of a bat with fur and a person with hair, or a bat mother with her pup and a human mother with her child. Have the children complete the project by writing a few sentences about his or her illustrations.

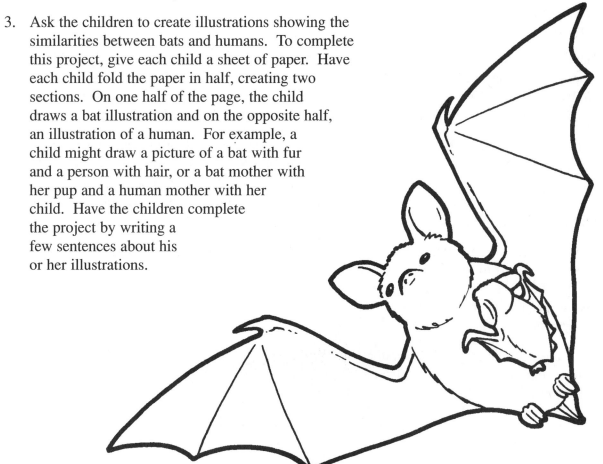

Hibernation

Hibernation means to spend the winter not being very active. Very few mammals actually hibernate. Bats are some of the few mammals that do. Not all bats hibernate, however. Those that live in climates that are warm all year do not need to hibernate. Bats that do hibernate sleep during the cold months of the year. During this deep sleep a bat's heart rate drops from 900 beats to only 20 beats per minute. Their breathing slows down, too.

Before hibernating bats spend the autumn months eating incredible amounts of food in order to increase their body weight. It is necessary for them to store body fat so that they can live on the fat during hibernation. This explains why some bats eat as many as 1,000 insects every hour during the summer and early fall.

In the United States, bats typically hibernate from October to March. They find peaceful places to sleep during these months such as caves, attics, hollow trees, or barns. It is important that they find undisturbed places to hibernate because if they wake up during the winter months too much of their body fat is used and the bats can die. Being disturbed just one time can cause a bat to burn a month's supply of fat. It is also important for bats to choose hibernation spots that are well above the ground. If they don't they can be eaten by foxes, rats, and other hungry creatures. When bats hibernate they often huddle together and wrap their wings around their bodies and ears. This helps them to stay warm. Hibernating bats sometimes appear to be dead because they rarely move. Bats don't always huddle together with their own bat colonies. Often bats from different colonies and even different species will snuggle together during hibernation.

Activities

1. Have the children discuss things animals and people do to keep warm in the winter. Record their responses on chart paper. Have the children huddle close to one another in a small, tight group for two minutes. Then have the children step away from each other and stand apart for two minutes. In which configuration did they feel the warmest? Huddled or standing apart? Why?

2. A bat's heart normally beats 900 times in a minute. Ask the children to count the number of times their hearts beat in one minute. (Have each child find his or her own pulse by gently placing the pointer and middle fingers of one hand on the side of his or her neck just underneath the jaw area.) How many more beats per minute does a bat's heart beat than the children's one-minute heart beat average?

3. Have the children research and discover other animals that hibernate in the winter. Make a classifying chart to record if the hibernating animal sleeps underground, on the ground, or above the ground. The children can draw illustrations of the animals to be added to the chart. You may also want to create the Creatures of the Night bulletin board suggestion on page 66 for added enjoyment.

4. Have the children take a "hibernation nap" after a noisy or busy activity to get them calmed down before your next lesson or learning experience.

What's Guano?

Guano is the manure of flying animals that is used for fertilizer. Believe it or not, bat fecal droppings have been proven to be extremely beneficial fertilizer. There is a large business in harvesting bat guano from bat caves and selling it as bagged fertilizer. The mining of guano is a primary form of income for some Third World countries.

In the caves of large bat colonies, guano covers the floor in thick layers (often times many feet deep). Bat guano has the consistency of flour and is home to microorganisms that have been proven beneficial to plants.

Activities

1. Ask the children to name what helps plants grow (water, sunlight, air, and soil). Explain that plants also need food, called fertilizer, in order to stay healthy. Discuss different types of fertilizer. (Some are made from plants like cotton and beets. Some are made from seaweed and algae. Others are made from the fecal droppings of animals.) Explain to the children that guano is the name for bat droppings and that guano is used as fertilizer. Show the children a bag of fertilizer from a local greenhouse. Decide if guano is a part of the ingredients listed.

2. Try an experiment to see how fertilizer helps plants stay healthy. Plant two identical plants or seeds. Periodically fertilize one of the two plants. (Use any kind of plant fertilizer if you do not have access to bat guano-enriched fertilizer.) Ask the children to make observations each week wherein they compare the growth and health of the two plants. Is one plant growing faster than the other one? Are the leaves of the two plants the same color? What other differences can be observed? Have the children record their observations on a group chart or individual recording sheets.

Where in the World?

Label the world map to show where these bats live.

Flying foxes and **Kitti's hog-nosed bats** (called **bumblebee bats**) live in Asia.

Bent-wing bats and **noctule bats** live in Europe.

Little brown bats and **Mexican free-tail bats** live in North America.

Spear-nosed bats and **wrinkle-faced bats** live in Central America.

46

Where in the World? Map

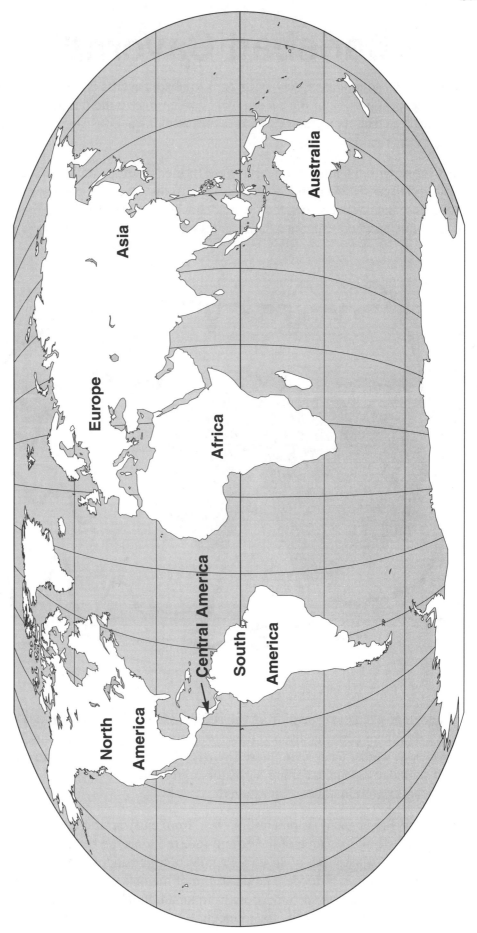

Carlsbad Caverns

Located in the Guadalupe Mountains of New Mexico, Carlsbad Caverns is a wonderland of stalagmites and stalactites. The deepest portion of the cavern that is accessible to the public extends 830 feet (253 meters) below the surface. The temperature of the cavern remains at consistent 56 degrees Fahrenheit (14 degrees Celsius) year-round.

The beautiful formations within Carlsbad Caverns were formed as drops of water seeped through cracks in the ground. The water passed over limestone causing it to dissolve. As particles of limestone were carried by the water into the cavern below, they were deposited in the form of calcite creating cave decorations that resemble curtains, columns, domes, and other interesting formations.

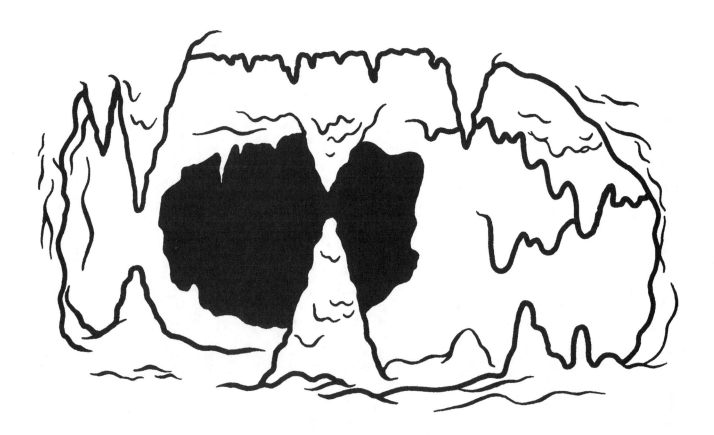

Stalactites are calcite deposits that suspend from the ceiling of the cave. Stalagmites extend up from the floor of the cave as calcite deposits dripped down with the water. To help your children remember the meaning of these two words, teach them these saying, "Stalactites stick *tight* to the ceiling," and "Stalagmites *might* someday reach the ceiling." Visitors to the cavern can go on three different tours of the cave to see these amazing mineral configurations.

Carlsbad Caverns is home to as many as one million bats from early spring to October. During the day, these nocturnal creatures sleep in an area of the cavern referred to as the bat cave. Three hundred bats often crowd together in one square foot of space. Each evening at sundown hundreds of thousands of adult bats leave the cave in search of food. The departure of the bats can last anywhere from twenty minutes to two hours and can be viewed by visitors from an amphitheater outside the cave's entrance. The bat cave itself is only open to scientists for research.

Bats of Carlsbad Caverns

Mexican free-tailed bats are the most prevalent bats in Carlsbad Caverns. They feed on insects and use echolocation to catch their prey. The bats from Carlsbad Caverns consume approximately 3,000 pounds of insects every night by flying out into the Southwestern desert areas surrounding the cave. Mexican free-tailed bats are gray or brown in color. They have long, narrow wings and a thin tail that dangles below their bodies.

Mexican free-tailed bats live in many places throughout the southern and western portions of the United States. The Mexican free-tailed bats that inhabit Carlsbad Caverns do so in the spring to mid-fall. They then migrate to the warmer climate of tropical Mexico for the winter months. While as many as seven other types of bats make their home in the cavern, the Mexican free-tailed bats are the most numerous.

The bat cave section of Carlsbad Caverns provides a safe home for the bats and also serves as a nursery for the bat babies, known as pups. Mother bats give birth to their young in the cave and raise them there until they are able to fly in late summer.

Mexican free-tail bats live in other caves in the Southwest. Thousands of them live in Eagle Creek Cave in Arizona. The largest colony of Mexican free-tailed bats lives in Bracken Cave near San Antonio, Texas. This cave is home to nearly 20 million Mexican free-tailed bats from spring to fall!

Sadly, the Mexican free-tail bat population has been decreasing in numbers over the past few years. Carlsbad Caverns use to have as many as 8 million Mexican free-tailed bats but now is home to only 250,000 bats. Eagle Creek Cave in Arizona used to have 30 million bats, but now houses only 30,000 bats. Many bat colonies have been reduced due to farmers' use of chemical pesticides, but human pillaging is an equally strong threat to the bats' survival. Some people find it game to fire shotgun shells into the colonies as they are roosting peacefully. This pillage has been one of the main reasons for the reduction of bats in the Eagle Creek Cave in Arizona.

Endangered!

Bats' Enemies

Bats do have natural enemies. Owls, hawks, snakes, and raccoons kill bats. Bats can also be killed when flood waters wash out caves where they are hibernating. The biggest danger to bats is from people. Pesticides that farmers use to kill bugs also kill the bats when they eat the infected bugs. Some people kill bats on purpose by shooting them. Other people kill bats by accident when they enter a bat cave in the winter and wake up hibernating bats. Waking up a hibernating bat can cause it to die.

Mexican Free-Tailed Bat

In Arizona, Eagle Creek Cave used to have more than 30 million bats living inside it. Now there are less than 30 thousand bats living in the cave.

Flying Fox Bat

This large bat is often killed for food for people to eat in Asian countries. Many kinds of flying fox bats are already extinct.

Let's Save Bats!

What do you think we should do to help protect and save the bats that are left in the world?

_____

_____

_____

Draw a picture on the back of this paper to illustrate what you think we should do.

Adopt-a-Bat

Your children can help save bats by adopting one through Carlsbad Caverns in New Mexico. Encourage the children to raise money to sponsor one or more of these endangered animals. The fee for adopting a bat is $6.

For joining the Carlsbad Caverns' Adopt-a-Bat program, your children will receive an adoption certificate, a brochure about bats, a bumper sticker, and a postcard of a Mexican free-tailed bat.

For more information contact:

Adopt-a-Bat
Carlsbad Caverns Guadalupe Mountains Association
P.O. Box 1417
Carlsbad, NM 88221

Or contact Carlsbad Caverns via the Internet at:

www.caverns.org/abat.htm

Tell the World

Encourage your children to spread the word about bats and bat conservation. Divide the children into groups of three or four and have them create short presentations on saving bats to share with other children. Your children may also want to create posters containing interesting bat facts and display the posters in the hallways or library. They may also want to design an information handout that can be distributed to other classes or to the community. Helpful bat Web sites (see pages 58 and 59) as well as information on adopting a bat (above) can be included in the information flyer.

Tissue-tube Bat

Materials

- newspaper
- half of a toilet tissue-paper tube
- black tempera paint
- paint brush
- 8"x5" (20cm x 13cm) sheet of black tissue paper
- two plastic wiggle eyes
- glue
- white tempera paint
- small, pointed-tip paintbrush

Directions

1. Spread newspaper onto the work surface.

2. Paint the cut tube with black paint; allow paint to dry thoroughly.

3. Twist the tissue paper tightly to make a thin rope. Thread the tissue paper through the hole in the tube.

4. Adjust the tissue paper so that equal amounts extend from each side. Gently untwist the tissue paper and spread apart to form the bat's wings.

5. Glue on the two plastic wiggle eyes.

6. Add a smile using the paintbrush and white paint.

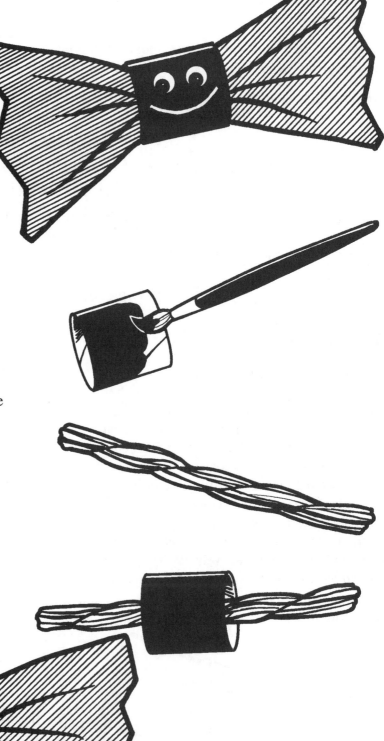

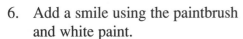

Windsock Bat

Materials

- two 12" x 18" (30 cm x 46 cm) sheets and one 9" x 13" (23 cm x 32 cm) sheet of black construction paper
- black plastic trash bag, precut to 9"x18" (23 cm x 46 cm)
- glue
- scissors
- hole punch
- stapler
- white crayon
- yarn

Directions

1. Position one 12" x 18" (30 cm x 46 cm) sheet of construction paper horizontally on a table.

2. Squeeze a trail of glue along the lower (longer) edge of the paper. Place one 18" (46 cm) edge of the precut plastic atop the glue; allow to dry.

3. Spread glue all over one side of the second piece of 12"x18" (30 cm x 46 cm) sheet of black construction. Place it atop the first sheet, aligning the edges and press firmly to seal the two sheets; allow to dry.

4. Roll the dried construction paper sheets into a tube shape and secure with staples. Be certain you only staple together the construction paper. Do not staple the hanging plastic.

5. Use sharp scissors to cut the hanging plastic into vertical one-inch (2.54 cm) strips.

6. From the smaller sheet of black construction paper, cut out two triangular bat wings by cutting the sheet in half diagonally.

7. Make a wing tab by folding in a tabbed section approximately ³/₄" (1.8 cm) along the short edge of each wing. Secure the tabbed wing to the bat with glue; allow to dry.

8. Use the white crayon to draw the bat's facial features. Make two holes on the opposite sides of the top portion of the tube using the hole punch. Tie the ends of your desired length of yarn in each hole to create a hanger.

Bats at Sunset

Materials

- newspaper
- one 9"x13" (23 cm x 32c m) sheet of black construction paper
- bat pattern cutouts (see Step 2 below)
- red, orange, and yellow tempera paint (in individual containers)
- three 2" (6 cm)-square sponge pieces, dampened
- masking tape

Directions

1. Cover the workspace with newspaper. Place the construction paper on the workspace.

2. Place two or three bat cutouts (reproduce and cut out a number of bats using the bat pattern below) in desired places on the construction paper by taping in place using small tape curls on the *underside* of each bat pattern.

3. Using the sponge squares (one sponge per paint color), dab red, yellow, and orange paint onto the paper to create a sunset scene. (The sponge-painting should overlap colors as well as overlap the edges of the bat cutouts.)

4. When the mixture of colors has created the desired sunset look, allow to dry. Remove the bat cutouts to reveal black bat silhouettes against the sunset sky.

bat pattern

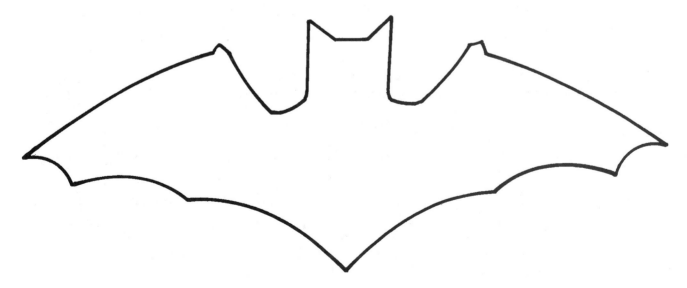

Sing a Song

When The Bats Go Flying In

(Sung to the tune of *When the Saints Go Marching In*)

Oh, when the bats go flying in,
Oh, when the bats go flying in,
—They'll eat the bugs that bother the farmers,
When the bats go flying in.
(Repeat chorus)
—They'll help to pollinate all the flowers,
 When the bats go flying in.
(Repeat Chorus)
—We won't be bothered by mosquitoes,
 When the bats go flying in.

Bats, Bats, Bats

(Sung to the tune of *Three Blind Mice*)

Bats, bats, bats.
Bats, bats, bats.
Flying in the night.
Oh, what a beautiful sight.
In the wintertime they hibernate,
In caves and trees they congregate.
We all know that bats are really great,
Those bats, bats, bats!

Bats Are Special

(Sung to the tune of *You Are My Sunshine*)

Bats are so special, they're really special,
But they're endangered throughout the world.
We need to save them—before it's too late,
Oh, please don't take these creatures away.

The Bats Are Flying

(Sung to the tune of *The Ants Go Marching*)

The bats are flying in the night, hoorah, hoorah!
They do their hunting without light, hoorah, hoorah!
The bats are eating all the bugs.
The farmers want to give them hugs.
So let's keep the bats safe—all through the year—have no fear—save the bats!

Write a Bat Song

Writing your own bat song is easy. Just choose a tune that you know and change the words. Finish the bat songs below. Then pick a different tune and write one of your own.

(Sung to the tune of *Twinkle, Twinkle, Little Star*)

Bats are _____ and bats are _____.

I think bats are really _____.

They are good at catching _____.

They sleep hanging _____.

Bats are _____ and bats are _____.

I think bats are really _____.

(Sung to the tune of *London Bridge*)

Bats are flying in the _____,

In the _____ , in the _____.

They eat _____ and they eat _____.

Bats are _____.

Now it's time for you to make up your own bat song using a familiar tune that you know. Write the name of the tune you will use on the line below and write out the verse or verses to your song on the back of this paper.

My tune is

_____

Batty Edibles

Fruit Bat Delight

Enjoy a fruit bat's favorite meal by creating a yummy fruit salad. Fruit bats eat a variety of fruit, including mangoes, bananas, guavas, grapes, and papayas. Some bats also eat citrus fruits, figs, and dates. Cut up and mix a variety of these fruits in a large bowl. Serve the salad to your children for a delightfully sweet bat treat.

Iced Bat Sugar Cookies

Using a standard sugar-cookie dough, have each child make a bat shape. This can be done easily by forming a flattened oval (body) and two flattened triangles (wings). On either side of the body, slightly overlap the wings and press the pieces together. Bake according to the recipe directions and allow the cookies to cool. Provide the children with brown icing (white frosting colored with food coloring) for spreading atop the cooled cookies. If desire, decorate the frosted cookies with candy sprinkles.

Batty Cupcakes

Bake any standard cupcake recipe using cupcake liners. Frost each cupcake with frosting that has been dyed brown with food coloring. Use gumdrops for the bat's ears, placing the gumdrops toward the top-back of the cupcake's "mound" of frosting. Add two chocolate-coated candy pieces for the eyes, placing them towards the front portion of the frosting "mound." Cut two pieces of fruit leather into the shape of wings and press them into the sides of the frosting mound.

Nocturnal Nectar

Allow your children time to decorate plain paper cups with flying bats using black permanent markers. Then fill the decorated cups with any flavor of fruit juice. When serving the fruit salad, sugar cookies, or batty cupcakes, encourage the children to sip on some nocturnal nectar between bites!

Batty Bake Sale

Make one, or all, of the delicious treats above to sell at a bake sale. Consider donating the proceeds from the sale to Adopt-a-Bat (page 51) or to Bat Conservation International (Web site, page 58). If your school prohibits the sale of homebaked goods, use store-bought items. During the fall season many grocery stores sell bat cupcakes, cookies, and other batty treats. Encourage your children to share information about bats with their bake-sale customers using either a formal (written) or informal (verbal) format.

Techno-Bats

Connect to the Internet and go batty over these bat sites!

Adopt-a-Bat
http://www.caverns.org/abat.htm

Are your children interested in adopting a bat (page 51)? If so, this Web site provides information about the Carlsbad Caverns Adopt-a-Bat program.

The Backyard Bat Page
http://www.webb-it.com/bats

The Backyard Bat is a delightful site filled with a large assortment of bat information, activities, research projects, and links. At this site, you can also subscribe to a free monthly e-mail newsletter. Past editions of The Backyard Bat Newsletter can be found at the following Web site:

http://www.webb-it.com/bats/bat_newsletter

Basically Bats: Stuff Just for Kids
http://www.lads.com/BasicallyBats/kids/

Hosted by Benny, the Big Brown Bat, this inviting Web site provides amusing illustrations, information, and activities. Also, check out the homepage of Basically Bats for even more information:

http://karst.lads.com/BasicallyBats/index.html

Bat Conservation International Homepage
http://www.batcon.org/

This Web site is loaded with information and links to such sites as educator's activities, BATS Magazine, FAQ sheets, plans for building bat houses, and even a site to hear bat echolocation sounds.

Bat Conservation International: Bat Facts and Amazing Trivia
http://www.batcon.org/trivia.html

At this Web site discover a variety of interesting bat facts from amazing feats to important information about bat life.

Techno-Bats *(cont.)*

The Buzbee Bat House Temperature Plot
http://www.nyx.net/~jbuzbee/bat_house.html

Along with bat house updates, this site offers a huge collection of bat links on subjects such as Bats Around the World, Bat Organizations, Bat Exhibits, Kids and Bats, and Bat Humor.

Canadian Wildlife Service
http://www.ec.gc.ca/cws-scf/hww-fap/bats/bats.html

This Web site, sponsored by the Canadian Wildlife Service, provides photographs of bats and information about how bats echolocate, what they eat, where they live, and much, much more. You will also find a suggested reading list of books about bats.

Organization for Bat Conservation
http://members.aol.com/obcbats/obchome.html

This Web site provides photos, bat sounds, information about bats, making bat houses, and echolocation.

The National Park Service: Carlsbad Caverns National Park
http://www.nps.gov/cave/

Connect to Carlsbad Caverns National Park's Web site for photographs of cave formations, general information, and the park's upcoming events.

The National Park Service: Watchable Wildlife in the National Parks
http://www.aqd.nps.gov/wv/caca_wwl.htm

This Web site provides photos of individual bats, as well as bats leaving Carlsbad Caverns for nightly hunting. You can also learn about other wildlife in Carlsbad Caverns and the surrounding New Mexico area.

Batty Scavenger Hunt

Connect to The Bat Conservation International Web site (http://www.batcon.org) and answer these questions.

1. People believe information about bats that is not true. Write an example of bat information that is not true.

   _____

2. Find a list of bat facts. What are two new facts that you have learned?

   _____

   _____

3. Find out how to build a bat house. What did you learn?

   _____

   _____

4. What are the names of three bats that live in the United States?

   _____

5. Find information about a bat called a flying fox. What did you learn?

   _____

6. Write two other things you have learned from this Web site.

   _____

   _____

A Batty Good Time

Enjoy one or all of these activities to culminate your children's learning experiences. A batty good time is best shared with friends!

Invitations

Invite parents, administrators, and/or children from other classes to join you in your culminating experiences. Duplicate and cut out the invitation squares on page 76. Duplicate and cut out the bat pattern on page 77. Glue the top square to one side of the bat pattern. Glue the bottom square to the back side of the pattern. Color the bat and add appropriate details to the backside information square (date, time, location) and deliver the completed invitations.

Bat Centers

Arrange your room with several centers for your shildren and/or guests to experience during the final day(s) of the bats unit. You may want to send invitations to the guests you will be inviting (see above). For the bat centers, choose activities that you have not already completed with your children or activities that your children would enjoy completing again with the guests. Some possible center activities are Tissue-tube Bat (page 52), Bats at Sunset (page 54), Write a Bat Song (page 56), Iced Bat Sugar Cookies or Batty Cupcakes (page 57), Nocturnal Nectar (page 57), and making a Big Book (page 73).

You're Up to Bat!

Test your children's or your guests' knowledge of bats by playing You're up to Bat! The gameboard and question/answer cards can be found on pages 69 through 71. Directions for making the gameboard, as well as how to play the game, can be found on page 16, #14.

Techno-Bats

If you have access to the Internet in your classroom, have children play Web site guides and show your guests some of the interesting bat Web sites (pages 58 and 59).

Batty Good Bites

Hopefully you have raised bat awareness in your school by having the children hold a bake sale (page 57) to raise funds for adopting bats (page 51). Now use some or all of the tasty treats as refreshments during your culminating experiences.

Bat House Book

Send your children and guests home with valuable information about building a bat house (instruction booklet, pages 62-64). (You may want to actually assemble a bat house in your room. Ask parents or other adults to donate the supplies and participate with the assembling process.)

Make a Bat House

If bats live in your area, your children may be interested in making a bat house for their own yards. If bats do not live in your area, you may want your children to make a bat house they can donate to Bat Conservation International (Web site, page 58). Have the children assemble Bat House books, which include simple building directions (pages 63 and 64). After coloring the pages of their little books, the children can take them home to make a bat house with their family or they can be used while building a bat house at school.

Folding Directions

Reproduce pages 63-64. Follow the folding illustrations below and staple the pages together near the left side edge of the assembled book to create the book's spine.

Bat House Book

L

Bats come out of hibernation in March. If bats come to live in your bat house, do not disturb them.

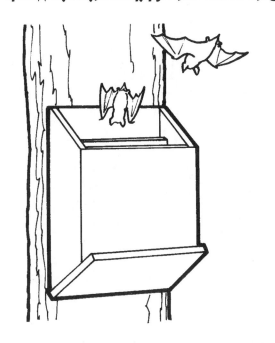

2

A simple bat house can be made out of wood and nails.

To learn more about bats, contact Bat Conservation International.

Address:

P.O. Box 162603
Austin, TX 78716

Web Site: www.batcon.org

8

How To Make A Bat House

With a little help, you can make a bat house for your backyard.

1

Bat House Book *(cont.)*

Here's another type of bat house. This one has screening on the backside of it. **3**

If you live where it is cold, hang your bat house in a sunny place. In warm climates, hang your bat house in a shady spot. **6**

Your bat house should be 2 feet (61 cm) tall. It should be 14 inches (42 cm) wide. The wood you use should be rough, not smooth.

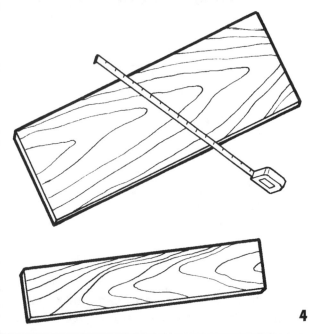

4

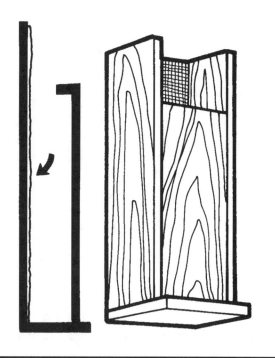

Hang your assembled bat house high on a tree. You can also hang it on the side of your house. **5**

Batty Bulletin Boards

Going Batty Over Poetry

This bulletin board is an eye-catching way to display your children's bat poetry. Design the background using gray or blue bulletin-board paper for the sky and brown paper to make a tree trunk and bare branches. Duplicate the bat pattern on page 77 for each child. Have each child turn a cutout bat pattern *upside-down* to write his or her poem on it. After the poem is written, the child then folds the bat's wings slightly over its body and attaches the bat (still upside-down) to one of the branches.

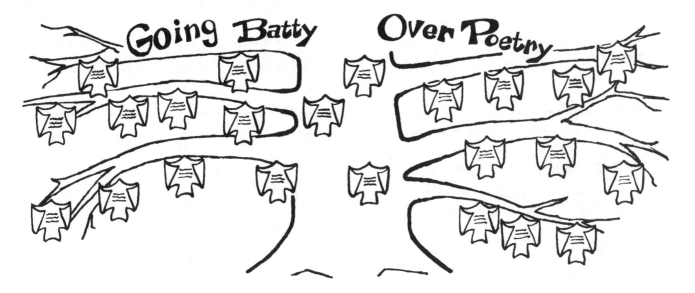

Not So Batty Facts

Create the background so that it looks like the inside of a cave, complete with stalactites and stalagmites. On reproduced bats (pattern, page 77), have the children write bat facts they have learned. Attach the bats randomly to the background.

Batty Bulletin Boards *(cont.)*

Creatures of the Night

As children learn about bats, encourage them to also learn about other nocturnal animals. Allow the children to use resource books, encyclopedias, and other materials to discover other animals that are most active at night. To create the bulletin board, cover the background with black bulletin-board paper (a handy alternative to using a standard bulletin board is to use the front of a door in your room). Provide paper, glue, scissors, and markers for the children. As they discover about other nocturnal animals, have them make the creatures out of construction paper and markers and attach the creatures to the board/door with identification labels. The children can also add a landscape to the black-sky background. The look of the added landscape will depend on where the pictured nocturnal animals live and sleep.

The Bat Cave

A designated corner of your room can be transformed into a bat-cave learning environment that your children are sure to enjoy.

Creating the Bat Cave

Designate a corner of your room for your bat-cave area. Position bookcases or dividers to create a mini-room. Leave a space for a small entrance (see Entering the Bat Cave below). If desired, cover the outside of the mini-room with brown, crinkled bulletin-board paper and label the area The Bat Cave.

Add to the Bat Cave

• Posters or magazine photos of bats, bat stuffed animals (Bibliography, page 79), and a world map

• Books about bats, caves, Carlsbad Caverns, stalagmites, and stalactites

• Megabat and Microbat Fact bats (pages 37 and 38), reproduced, cut out, and attached to the inside of the "cave" walls

• Any other desired bat-related materials, games, or activities

• A sign-in sheet and a pencil attached to a clipboard

Entering the Bat Cave

The bat cave can be set up as a free-time or planned center area, a reading corner, or as an incentive for children's good behavior. For use as a behavior incentive, duplicate and cut apart the bat coupons on page 68. Distribute the bat coupons to children who exhibit positive behavior or good citizenship. When a child collects a predetermined number of coupons, he or she trades them in and gets to enter the bat cave for a predetermined amount of time.

When a child enters the bat cave, he or she signs in and then spends a relaxing predetermined number of minutes browsing through the information and materials in the cave. When the child is ready to leave the cave, he or she signs out. At the end of each day, have an assigned child check the sign-in sheet (or you can check the sheet yourself). Those children who were first-time visitors that day are awarded a duplicated bat badge and certificate (page 68).

Bat-Cave Coupons

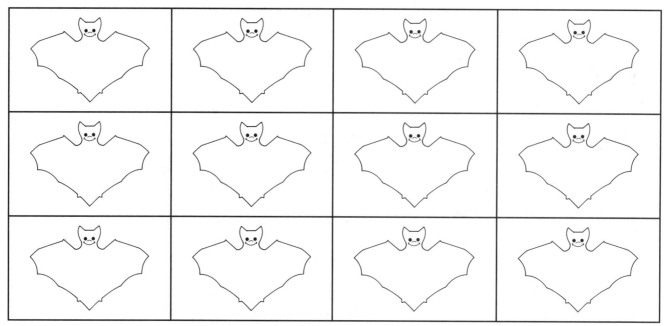

Badge

Certificate

I'm batty about bats!

_____

(Child's Name)

is

b a t t y

about

BATS!

You're up to Bat! Questions

How many babies does a mother bat have each year?	What does a mother bat do with her baby when it flies?	What does nocturnal mean?
What do most flying foxes eat?	Why do bats wrap their wings around themselves?	What is echolocation?
How do microbats see in the dark?	Why do most bats have big ears?	What enemies do bats have?
What do most bats do in the winter?	Do vampire bats live in the United States?	What do vampire bats eat?
Why are bats endangered?	Do most bats have rabies?	What is a baby bat called?
Where do bats sleep?	Should you ever touch a bat?	Are there more megabats or microbats?
What is strange about the way bats sleep?	What is guano?	How are bats like birds?
How do bats help farmers?	What is bat guano used for?	How are bats different from birds?
Are bats blind?	What is the wingspan of the biggest bat?	Do megabats like warm or cold weather?
Do bats attack people?	What do bats feed their babies?	Are all bats black?

You're up to Bat! Gameboard

10	20	30
10	20	30
10	20	30
10	20	30
10	20	30
10	20	30
10	20	30
10	20	30
10	20	30
10	20	30

You're up to Bat! Answers

active at night	she carries it	one or two
using sound waves to find objects	to keep warm	fruit
owls, hawks, raccoons, snakes, people	to hear better	they use echolocation
blood	no	hibernate
a pup	no	pesticides and people
microbats	no	caves, trees, barns, and buildings
they have wings; some eat bugs	bat droppings	they sleep upside down
they are mammals; no feathers; sleep upside down	fertilizer	they eat bugs
warm	six feet	no
no	milk	no

Bat Wing Pattern

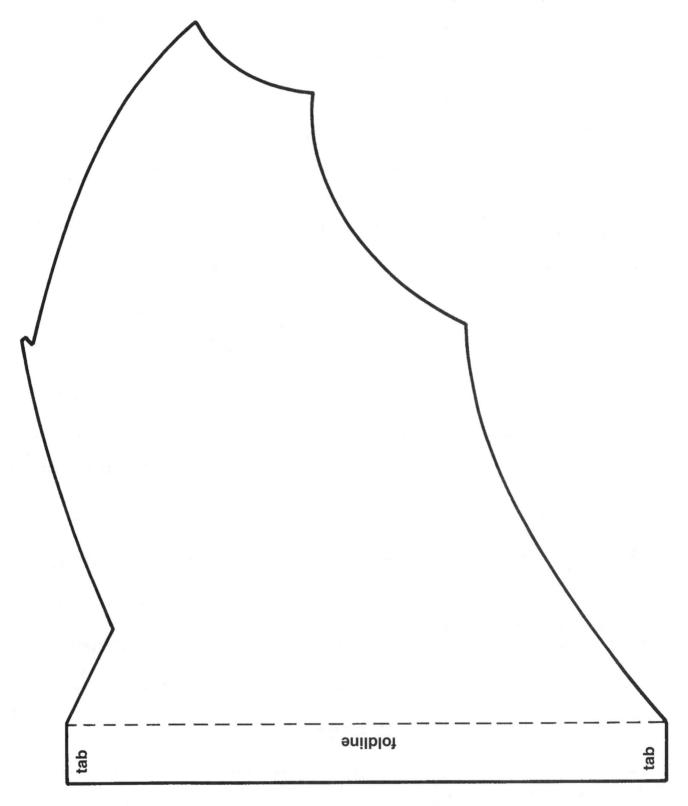

tab

foldline

tab

Note: To make one pair of wings, reproduce bat wing pattern onto two pieces of dark grey or black construction paper; cut out wings. Turn one of the wings over (as if you were opening a book). You will now have a left and a right wing.

Making a Big Book

Big books are a wonderful language arts experience that combines reading, writing, speaking, listening, and encourages artistic creativity.

Steps

1. Before making the big books, gather all of the children into one group and review the types of bats studied and bat facts they have learned. Brainstorm or review a list of vocabulary words that might be useful when writing the big books, such as echolocation, microbat, megabat, and nocturnal.

2. Provide each child or cooperative group (group size should not exceed four children) with five large sheets of paper (at least 12" x 18" [30 cm x 46 cm]). One sheet will serve as the book's cover. The children may write a title on the cover first or choose to wait until the remainder of their book is completed.

3. On each of the remaining four sheets (pages), the children feature one particular bat per page. Information learned about the four bats is written at the bottom of each page and an illustration of each bat is drawn above the written information. (If possible, try not to assign any children the same bats.)

   If desired, for younger children, duplicate the bat clip art (pages 74 and 75) for the children to use in their books. They can cut out the reproduced bats, glue them onto the book pages, and draw background illustrations. The children can then dictate their desired text to an adult who in turn can write the shared information on each page.

4. Have the children or an adult stack the completed pages in correct sequence (title page followed by the four bat information pages), align the edges, and staple the pages together along the left side edge to create the book's spine.

5. Encourage the children to read their bat fact books to one another. If desired, have the children share their big books with other children during library time or by visiting other children's classrooms.

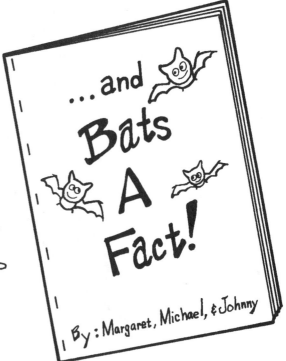

Big Book Bat Clip Art

Hog-nosed Bat

Little Brown Bat

     74

Big Book Bat Clip Art *(cont.)*

Flying Fox

Long-eared Bat

Rulers and Invitation

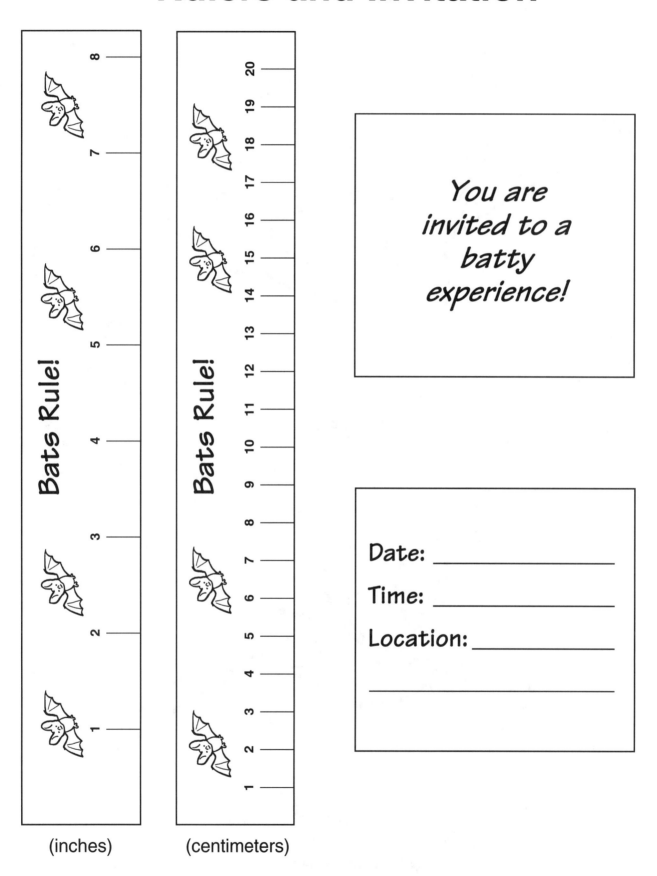

(inches)   (centimeters)

You are invited to a batty experience!

Date: _____

Time: _____

Location: _____

_____

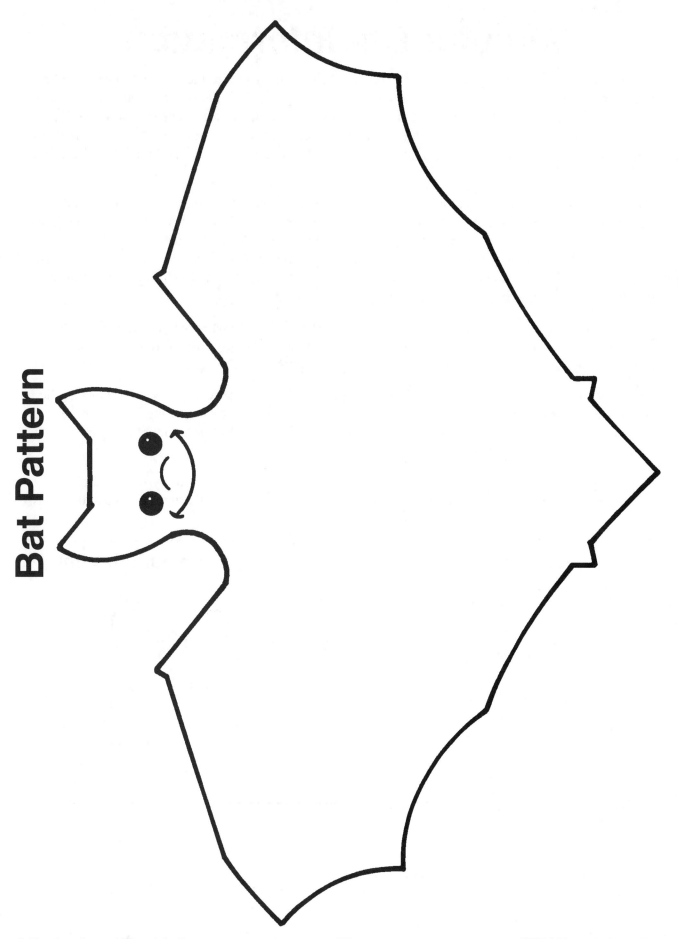

Bat Pattern

Vampire Bat Information

The look and name of vampire bats may frighten your children. Vampire bats are the most feared bats because they feed on blood. In fact, they are the only bats that feed on the blood of other animals. Vampire bats have very sharp teeth. They use their front teeth to trim away feathers and fur of a sleeping animal. Then they use sharp fang-like teeth to make a small cut in animals' skin. The bats do not literally suck the blood from animals, they use their tongues to lap up the blood that flows from the cuts.

Vampire bats feed at night on the blood of horses, cows, and sometimes, people. They rarely disturb their victims. Vampire bats find a sleeping animal, hop gently onto its body to find a place to feed, and then nestle in for a meal. The saliva of vampire bats contains a chemical that keeps blood from clotting. This chemical helps keep the blood flowing out of the animals while the bats feed. Scientists are studying this chemical to see if it can be used to help heart patients. This helpful chemical may be able to prevent clotting in human blood and prevent heart attacks.

One concern many people have is that these blood-drinking mammals can spread diseases that will make their victims sick or die. That may be true, but the opposite is also true. Vampire bats can contract diseases from sick animals or people. If the bats contract fatal diseases they can die, too.

Vampire bats often help each other to survive. If vampire bats do not eat every few days they can die, therefore well-fed vampire bats will often feed hungry vampire bats by regurgitating blood for the hungry bats to drink. Vampire bats help in other ways, too. They are known to adopt and care for orphaned baby bats.

Some types of bats are called false vampire bats. One such bat is called the woolly false vampire. These bats do not drink the blood of animals. Instead, they eat small animals such as mice and lizards.

vampire bat   woolly false vampire bat

Bibliography

Fiction

Cannon, Janell. *Stellaluna*. Harcourt Brace & Company, 1993.

Freeman, Don. *Hattie, the Backstage Bat*. Puffin Books, 1980.

Scholastic. *The Magic School Bus: Going Batty*. Scholastic, 1996.

Nonfiction

Appelt, Kathi. *Bats Jamboree*. Morrow Junior Books, 1996.

Earle, Ann. *Zipping, Zapping, Zooming Bats*. HarperCollins, 1995.

George, Michael. *Bats*. The Child's World, 1991.

Grasser, Linda. *Beautiful Bats*. Millbrook Press, 1997.

Gray, Susan Heinrichs. *A New True Book: Bats*. Children's Press, 1994.

Greenway, Frank. *Amazing Bats*. Alfred A. Knopf, 1991.

Kellogg, Steven. *The Island of the Skog*. Dial. 1993.

Lobe, Arnold. *Frog and Toad are Friends*. HarperCollins. 1979.

Lollar, Amanda. *The Bat in My Pocket*. Capra Press, 1992.

Lovett, Sarah. *Extremely Weird Bats*. John Muir Publications, 1991.

Maestro, Betsy. *Bats: Night Fliers*. Scholastic, 1994.

Pringle, Laurence. *Batman: Exploring the World of Bats*. Charles Scribner's Sons Books for Young Readers, 1991.

Pringle, Laurence. *Vampire Bats*. William Morrow & Co., 1982.

Tuttle, Merlin D., and Henley, D.L. *The Bat House Builder's Handbook* (Rev. Ed.). Bat Conservation International, 1996.

Software

Stellaluna. Living Books. Broderbund Software. 1997. Call 1-800-521-6263 (specifically ask for the Teacher's Edition), or for more information visit their Web site: www.broderbund.com

Toys

Stellaluna. Distributed by Harcourt Brace and Jovanivich. Manufactured by MerryMakers. 1994. ISNB 0-15-200286-3. This adorable stuffed toy has Velcro® attachments so that Stellaluna can wrap her wings around her body as well as hang upside-down from a child's finger or a small tree branch.

Long-Nosed Bat stuffed animal and *Cactus Café* literature book by Kathleen Weidner Zoefield. Soundprints. 1997. 1-800-228-7839.

JEROME LIBRARY
CURRICULUM RESOURCE CENTER
BOWLING GREEN STATE UNIVERSITY
BOWLING GREEN, OHIO 43403

Answer Key

Page 9

1. Mother and Stellauna were attacked by an owl.
2. Stellaluna fell into a bird nest.
3. Mother bird fed Stellaluna.
4. Stellaluna and the baby birds learned to fly.
5. Stellaluna found her mother.
6. Stellaluna protected and saved her bird friends.

Page 17

1. they eat them
2. they eat the bugs
3. grasshoppers, beetles, and moths
4. 600 mosquitoes or 150 bugs
5. accept any reasonable answer

Page 19

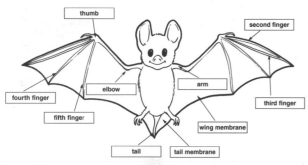

Page 26

Across	Down
1. predator	2. roost
6. nocturnal	3. membrane
8. hibernate	4. mammal
9. maneuver	5. sonar
10. colony	7. prey
12. insectivorous	11. echolocation

Bonus: Stellaluna

Page 27

1. false (bats are not blind)
2. true
3. true or false (some rocks are not hard)
4. true
5. true or false (some candy is sour)
6. true
7. true
8. true
9. true or false (some buttons may not appear cute)
10. false (a drink is not a living thing, therefore it is capable of emotion)
11. true
12. true
13. true or false (some trees are not tall)
14. true or false (sheets are not always white)

Page 28

1. fact
2. opinion
3. fact
4. fact
5. opinion
6. opinion
7. opinion
8. fact
9. opinion
10. fact
11. fact
12. opinion
13. opinion
14. fact

Page 35

1. 600 bats; 1,500 bats
2. 3 bats
3. 10 fingers; 80 fingers
4. 22 degrees F; 12 degrees C
5. 300 insects
6. 200 megabats
7. 14 babies
8. 4 inches; 18 centimeters
9. 180 miles
10. 15 years

Page 41

1. long-nosed bat
2. horseshoe bat
3. tube-nosed bat
4. hog-nosed bat
5. sword-nosed bat
6. leaf-nosed bat

er Created Materials, Inc.